HELLBOUND!

CANCELED!

McDougal & Associates
Servants of Christ and Stewards of the Mysteries of God

HELLBOUND!

CANCELED!
MY REAL-LIFE STORY

MARTY PEREZ

Hellbound! Cancelled!
Copyright © 2022—Martin Perez
ALL RIGHTS RESERVED

Unless otherwise noted, all Scripture references are from the
Holy Bible, King James Version, public domain.

Published by:

McDougal & Associates
18896 Greenwell Springs Road
Greenwell Springs, LA 70739
www,ThePublishedWord.com

McDougal & Associates is dedicated to spreading the Gospel
of the Lord Jesus Christ to as many people as possible in the
shortest time possible.

ISBN: 978-1-950398-64-5

Printed on demand in the U.S., the U.K.,
Australia and the UAE.
For Worldwide Distribution

Dedication

I want to dedicate this book to the memory of my mom:

Angelita Ramon Perez

She may not have been the ideal mom, but she did what she had to do to survive and feed her children. She went through Hell and back with my dad but never stopped being a provider and a mom at the same time. Beg, borrow, or steal, she got it done!

She's been gone for about three years now, and I miss her very much. I know that some day I'll see her again because she also gave her life to the Lord some years before her passing. I love you, Mom!

Contents

Foreword by Donald Gibson 9
Foreword by Pastor Haroldo Arevalo 13
Foreword by Myra (Perez) Ramirez 15

Introduction 21

1. My Earliest Memories 25
2. A New Start in Calallen 29
3. The Saga Continues 33
4. Learning the Drug Trade 37
5. Continued Exposure to the Worst Possible Things 41
6. The Good News and the Bad 45
7. Addicted Like My Elders....................................... 49
8. Keeping All the Wrong Company 53
9. A Close Call 57
10. Recovering My Money 61
11. A Stolen Computer 65
12. A Bank Robbery? 69

13. Uncle Benito's Plight 73
14. Plans to Kill Me 77
15. Arrested in Arkansas.. 81
16. Organized Crime 85
17. Where Was I?.. 89
18. Closing In.. 93
19. Who Came into My Cell?... 97
20. Spending Time Mopping the Hall 101
21. Attending a Spanish-Speaking Church 105
22. A Well-Organized Church... 109
23. Doing Evangelism.. 113
24. Getting to Know Carmen... 117
25. A New Ministry out of the Rubble................................... 121
26. Hombres al Maximo... 125
27. Why I Wrote the Book.. 129
28. That Terrible Crime 133
29. In Closing... 137

Author Contact Information... 138

Foreword by Donald Gibson

The saying goes, "Live what you preach." I honestly think that saying should be "Preach what you have lived!" And that is what Marty Perez does in this new book.

We are all "Hell-bound" without Jesus, and it is the turnaround from Hell-bound to Heaven-bound that gives credibility to the message of encouragement, redemption, and hope that God has placed in every born-again child of God. The Bible is made up of stories of redeemed people, who, if redemption had not happened, would have lived tragic lives:

- Both Joseph and Daniel were slaves whom God redeemed and promoted.
- Moses was a murderer who turned deliverer.

Marty Perez

- Ruth was a widow with no hope who became a part of the lineage of Jesus.
- Esther was a victim of sex trafficking, so to speak, but through redemption, God elevated her to a place of great prominence for the salvation of many of her people.

History, to the believer, the person who has committed their life to Christ, becomes His-story lived in us and through us. It is His-story that gives our story credibility, authority, and the impact of hope this world so desperately needs. The book you are about to read is such a story of redemption—from incarceration to redemption, restoration, and hope.

Many people find themselves incarcerated today, not all behind the bars of a cell, but behind their many hurts, fears, doubts, and brokenness. Maybe you have been trapped in a cell called failure, one called shame, or one called guilt. Within this story, you will find keys to unlock your cell and be introduced to the freedom that only comes through knowing Christ.

This book is not just another story to be told; it is a man who is telling what he has lived, which is the greatest sermon we could ever preach to a world around us looking for help and hope. As you turn each page, I pray it will be as if you are taking a step out of the prison life has tried to keep you in and into the glorious light of Christ.

Free people free people. So, as you turn the pages, let the freedom expressed in these pages, bring you to your own place of freedom and forgiveness. As a pastor, I'm so pleased that Marty is one of our own.

Donald Gibson
Pastor, MercyGate Church
Mont Belvieu, Texas

FOREWORD BY PASTOR HAROLDO AREVALO

Jesus Christ forgives, transforms, and gives us new life. What a marvelous truth that is worthy of never forgetting.

In my thirty-five years of service to the Body of Christ as a pastor, I've seen many men transformed by the power of God. My dear friend, Marty Perez, is one of the most impactful examples I've ever known.

In the pages of this book, you will read of one of the greatest miracles that God can accomplish for those who seek Him with all their heart. Marty's story of pain, suffering, sin, and wrongdoing for some years could not compare with the transformation and life change he has experienced through Jesus Christ.

Marty Perez

I know God is going to use this story to encourage you to look for your own miracle in Him.

Haroldo Arevalo
Pastor at Verbo Church
Westbank, New Orleans

Foreword by Myra (Perez) Ramirez

It's hard to believe anyone can truly change in the world we live in. A tiger can't change its stripes. Once a cheater, always a cheater. You know the sayings. The thing is: people can't change alone, BUT with God, all things are possible.

For most of my life, I both loved and feared the man whose story you're about to read. I always knew he loved me, that he would do anything to provide for and protect me. But I also knew that there was a monster there, a monster who came out at the same time the twelve pack did.

Although I was never physically hurt by this man, I saw the pain he was capable of inflicting, most often on my mom. This led to a fear and a hate that would intertwine with love until I was in my 30s.

This story is a tragic one. I didn't know most of the details written here until I was allowed to read a rough draft of the book. In retrospect, things make so much more sense now that I know what was going on behind the scenes of some of my earliest memories. Of course, there was no way I could have known them then.

We all have a story, some worse than others. The beautiful thing is this: we also have a God who has mercy on us and loves us despite our sins and mistakes. I can say with one hundred percent certainty that this devil of a man who was once of the world has truly been changed by a God who can.

As a matter of fact, I've seen God change both of my parents. And, because of the incredible work that's been done in my dad's life, he has been able to help so many other people. After years of anger and hurt, our relationship has been restored, and I'm so thankful that he's still alive today.

Hellbound! Cancelled!

If you're reading this, and you think there's no way that God can love you or forgive you for the things you've done, I'm here to reassure you that YES, HE CAN. If He can give my dad a whole new life, a reason to live and a goal to achieve, He can and He will help you too. All you need to do is ask Him.

Myra Ramirez

To those who are the called, both Jews and Greeks, Christ the power of God and the wisdom of God. For the foolishness of God is wiser than mankind, and the weakness of God is stronger than mankind. For consider your calling, brothers and sisters, that there were not many wise according to the flesh, not many mighty, not many noble; but God has chosen the foolish things of the world to shame the wise, and God has chosen the weak things of the world to shame the things which are strong, and the insignificant things of the world and the despised God has chosen, the things that are not, so that He may nullify the things that are, so that no human may boast before God.

1 Corinthians 1:24-29, NASB

> **HOW COULD A HOLY AND LOVING GOD TAKE SOMEONE WHO WAS THE SCUM OF THE EARTH AND TURN THEM INTO HIS OWN MASTERPIECE?**

Introduction

Born to an alcoholic mother who would beg, borrow, and steal (and even prostitute herself, if necessary) to provide for her children, and a drug-addicted father, and exposed in early life to violence, pornography, witchcraft, and homosexuality, just to name a few, I was called upon to start helping my dad with his drug trade as a very young boy. When he went to prison, I smuggled drugs to him to sell inside when I was just eleven. By the time I was in fourth and fifth grades, I was already having sex with both boys and girls. It is no wonder that upon dropping out of school and running away with a girl at fifteen to start a new life for the two of us in Dallas, Texas, all I knew was crime. Like my elders before me, I was soon addicted to a life of alcohol, drugs, partying, crime, and violence. In short, I was bound for Hell, and there didn't seem to be anything that could stop me.

Thankfully, that was not the end of my story. Many of my violent associates were killed, overdosed on drugs, or died of alcohol and drug abuse. Somehow I escaped every threat, and then one day my sentence was somehow suddenly canceled altogether. This is my story.

My name is Marty Perez. I was born in Robstown, Texas, on January 2, 1964. My dad, Dario "El Morro" Perez, was from the barrio of San Pedro in Robstown, and my mom, Angelita "Gela" Ramon Perez, was from a good family on Main Street. I say "good family" because Mom's brothers were all hard working and led decent lives. Dad and his brothers, on the other hand, were mostly into crime, violence, drugs, and alcohol. Two of them were fairly decent. One was in the U.S. Army, and the other was a truck driver.

Robstown was not the ideal place to be born or to live. Often called "Little Chicago," it was "the hood," and we and our neighbors all experienced the worst of it.

In the 60s, my sisters, Ida and Terrie, and my brother Tommy and I lived with our mother. My cousin Joe, who was like a brother to me, was (and still is) part of our life.

By 1969 my parents were divorced. Mom moved on with her life, while Dad was in and out of prison. In 1970 we moved to Houston. There mom remarried and gave birth to my youngest sister, Carolina.

By 1972 Mom had divorced Carolina's dad, and we moved back to Robstown. Out of prison, Dad got back with Mom, but it never lasted very long. Even though they tried over and over again throughout the years, it was to no avail. They just could not get along for very long.

During this time my siblings and I were exposed to the worst of the worst, but that is not my reason for writing the book. In this book, I want to share real-life experiences in order to bring hope to many who have gone through or maybe are even now going through similar circumstances.

Yes, there is hope for hurting victims, and there is also hope for people like me who committed heinous crimes. You see, although my life as a child and young adult was horrific, it had a happy ending. And that is the point I want to drive home in these pages.

As I write this introduction and pray for those who will read these words, I already know by the tears in my eyes that this book will be a blessing to many. My tears are not because of bad memories, but rather, tears of gratitude to the One Who brought me through it all. Praise God for our Lord Jesus Christ!

Marty Perez

Chapter 1

My Earliest Memories

Growing up in Robstown, my earliest memories are of spending time at my grandma, Ama Tonia's, house. In the late 1960s and early 70s, most of my mom's siblings and their kids would go there for Christmas. I think those were the most pleasant times in my early childhood.

In contrast, during that same period, I also remember living at a family house on Avenue C, and there I remember my parents having frequent barroom brawls. Mom says I would cut Dad's leg with a razor blade to make him stop beating her. I was about four at the time.

While we were living at this home, Dad went to prison, and we were left alone again.

Marty Perez

One night a man came knocking at the door very late. Mom hid us in another room and told us to be quite. She didn't answer the door, so the man eventually left, only to return on foot. We could hear him as he approached the back of the house, but then there was silence.

Then, suddenly, we heard a dog barking and someone trying to come through the wooden sub-floor. Mom told us that she knew who this man was and that he was demon possessed. We were experiencing the first of many encounters with witchcraft and the occult.

Mom and Ama Tonia had many friends who were into voodoo and witchcraft. Mom herself participated in many demonic rituals in those years. By the time Dad got out of prison this time, we were living in a tiny house next door to my Aunt Anita.

I have to give credit to my two aunts, Mom's sisters, Anita and Bertha. They were devout Catholic women, and they tried to teach us how to pray. It just didn't stick.

There, in that little house next door to Aunt Anita, the barroom brawls resumed. Older now, I had graduated to an empty Vodka bottle as my weapon of choice to defend Mom. Since she was an alcoholic, and Dad was addicted to heroin, I knew that at any given moment a fight could break out, so I slept with that bottle under my pillow.

One time the fight was so bad that Mom grabbed the Vodka bottle herself and took a swing at Dad. He moved away, and she missed. Unfortunately, I was standing right by her, and she ended up breaking the bottle on my face. It was 1969. I survived, and soon Mom divorced Dad, and we moved to Houston.

Mom''s new marriage also ended in divorce, and we moved back to Robstown, but we brought back a new addition to our family—little Carolina. This time Mom managed to hustle her way into buying a house in Calallen, a very nice suburb of Corpus Christi. This area had a completely different atmosphere. Things were looking up for us.

THINGS WERE LOOKING UP FOR US!

Chapter 2

A New Start in Calallen

Because Mom bought the house in Calallen, my siblings and I started school there. I was in third grade at the time. Dad continued to come and go as usual, and their party lifestyle was unchanged. Friends and family would often sleep over because some of the parties they attended lasted all night.

By the time I was in fourth and fifth grades, I was having sexual encounters with the kids of the other partygoers. Why? Because, most of the time, we children were left alone while our parents went out together and partied.

As weird as it sounds, I don't ever remember my dad ever taking us out to dinner or a movie, or ever saying, I love you. He did take us out to an occasional dance or two. We would sit around the table while the adults danced and drank.

Dad would also use me to go see one of his girlfriends. He would tell mom he was taking me along to run errands. Then we would drive to the lady's apartment, and I would wait for him in the car. I never told Mom about these encounters because I knew it would cause another fight, and Mom would end up with a beating.

One of the times my parents took me to a tejano dance with them, things went bad. Between sets, Dad went to the back where the band was. I'm assuming there were girls there too because Mom ended up in the back, and an argument started.

Dad physically forced Mom out the back door into the rear parking lot. But she was no pushover, so she fought back. As usual, I followed behind Mom to protect her. When I saw Dad pull out a gun and cock it, I jumped on a car and from its roof managed to hit him on the head with a beer bottle. When he saw blood gushing down his face, he stopped beating mom, and the fight was over—for the moment.

I don't know what happened after that because I had run inside and hid behind the bar. That was probably the last time Dad would bring me along. He just couldn't shake me. I was terribly frightened, but at least I saved Mom's life that day!

Wow! God was with us, even though we were not saved yet. Praise the Lord!

> **God was with us, even though we were not saved yet!**

Chapter 3

The Saga Continues

After a few days, life got back to normal. My parents kissed and made up. Both of them were hairstylists, but they also both did odd jobs at various times to make ends meet. More than anything, Dad was a drug trafficker and drug dealer.

In the early 1970s, it was fairly easy to smuggle drugs from Mexico to Corpus Christi. Mom's house had a single-car garage, so Dad would park cars loaded with drugs in that garage, one at a time, so we could unload them.

The car doors on the right side were hard to open due to lack of space, so Dad would have me and my little brother Tommy pull the drugs from the right side door panels because it was too tight for an adult to fit into.

Back then, weed was wrapped in butcher paper, and sometimes the paper tore when pulling the packets out of the door panels. Dad would pay us for helping by letting us keep whatever spilled from the torn packages. With what I got, I would fill plastic sandwich bags and then sell them in Robstown for $2 each. That was training ground for me and Tommy. He was nine at the time, and I was between ten and eleven.

The party lifestyle of our parents continued, and we children were often left alone. At this age, I was sexually molested by a boy a couple of years older than me. This boy, his mom, and his siblings were staying with us for a while. So, at ten and eleven years of age, I was already having sex with boys (and girls) around my same age. Parents, be careful who you leave your kids with!

PARENTS, BE CAREFUL WHO YOU LEAVE YOUR KIDS WITH!

Hellbound! Cancelled!

Once again, Dad got himself caught in a drug deal and went back to federal prison. By this time, he figured that I was capable of drug trafficking, and so he got me started. Mom would take me to Robstown, or I would find some other way to go. There I would buy a half-pound of weed to take to the prison where Dad was incarcerated. At that very young age, I had been promoted to drug trafficking.

CHAPTER 4

LEARNING THE DRUG TRADE

Before my first drug run, mom taught me and Tommy how to package the weed to make it ready for delivery. The three of us would place seven grams of weed in a plastic sandwich bag. Then we would put duct tape around the bag and place it inside a small balloon. After we tied the knot in the balloon, the package looked like a wiener for a hotdog.

Mom packed the drugs and some clothes for me and took me to the bus station in Corpus Christi. I would ride the bus five hundred miles by myself from Corpus to Texarkana. I was eleven!

Right now, I need to take a short pause because I'm just sobbing. Thank God that He got me through that hell.

Okay, I'm back.

When my bus arrived in Texarkana, a Columbian lady would pick me up at the station and drive me to her house. The next morning, she would strap the drugs on my body and drive me to the prison, where her husband was also doing time. She walked with me through the metal detectors, as I smuggled the drugs into the prison. Then, I would sit and wait for my dad, and she would wait for her visit with her husband. This was around 1973.

The inmates used the same rest room as the visitors. Dad would instruct me on who to give the drugs to when I went into the rest room. I gave them to two or three different men, and they would put the wieners up inside their body to get them back into the cellblocks. After I had safely delivered the drugs to Dad's men, I would go back and sit and visit with him. Very quickly, at that young age, I became fearless!

> **VERY QUICKLY, AT THAT YOUNG AGE, I BECAME FEARLESS!**

Hellbound! Cancelled!

The next day the Columbian lady would drop me off at the bus station and send me back to Corpus Christi. Once home, trying to be a normal kid, I would hang out with friends at my grandma's house in Robstown. Those kids also had parents like mine, so together we were always getting into trouble.

We would steal candies and goodies from the neighborhood stores or local 7-11. One time we climbed the roof of the Gulf Movie Theatre for some odd reason. We went up the wall from the Dollar Store. Once we were on the roof, one of my friend's feet got stuck in a hole. We looked through the hole and could see everything down inside the Dollar Store. We took off a big aluminum vent and went down. Then we proceeded to fill paper bags with candy and toys. That experience only gave us more boldness and ideas for future crimes.

THAT EXPERIENCE ONLY GAVE US MORE BOLDNESS AND IDEAS FOR FUTURE CRIMES!

Chapter 5

Continued Exposure to the Worst Possible Things

At twelve and thirteen, my friends would go into topless bars and help us sneak in too. What was worse, Dad's brothers left their Playboy magazines on the bathroom floor where any of us could see them. Today it is way easier for kids to see porn. Please monitor what your kids are watching.

Parents, be aware of what your kids log on to!

Dad would eventually be released from prison and come home again. But again, the vicious cycle continued. By this time Mom had gone through so many boyfriends I could hardly count them. Of course, Dad was always a player himself, so they were always fighting about who was playing whom.

As usual, Dad beat Mom up when he was high, but this time she was fed up with it. A few days after their last fight, he tried to come home to sweet-talk Mom. It had always worked for him before, but this time his words would fall to the ground, and so would he.

When Dad pulled into the driveway, Mom was waiting for him outside with a 22-caliber pistol in her hand. She told him to go away, and she pointed the gun at him. Dad just laughed at her.

Still mocking her, he began walking toward her. Mom pulled the trigger and hit him right in the gut.

After Dad had cried like a baby and begged Mom to call an ambulance, she finally gave in and called 911. He was rushed to Riverside Hospital, where the doctors did immediate surgery on him to stop the internal bleeding, and they were able to save his life. Dad told the cops it had been a drive-by shooting.

I wish I could say that the vicious cycle of violence ended that day, but it didn't. My parents kept at it off and on for years to come, but at least it was much less intense now.

At fifteen, I decided to transfer back to Robstown, where I attended Seale Junior High. That was a big mistake. I did it for all the wrong reasons. I had fallen for a girl from Robstown and wanted to be closer to her.

In the end, we both dropped out of school in the eighth grade and ran off together. We headed to Dallas where we hoped to start a new life.

By the time we were both seventeen, my girlfriend gave birth to our first daughter, Myra. I believe that day in April of 1981, when Myra was born, was the first time

Marty Perez

I had ever felt real love. Before that day, I don't remember ever feeling loved or giving love in that same capacity. Myra had captured my heart.

Myra had captured my heart!

Chapter 6

The Good News and the Bad

The good news is that right around this time (it was 1981), my parents' vicious cycle of violence finally came to an end. The bad news is that a new vicious cycle would begin between me and Myra's mom. Our lifestyle was identical to my parents, if not worse. I had corrupted her.

For the next twelve years or so, we fought, cheated on each other, and consumed large quantities of drugs and alcohol. This was the same satanic cycle my parents had experienced.

This type of cycle can never be broken by human wisdom or counseling. Programs might help for a while, but they will never sever the root of the problem. It takes the Word of God through the power of the Holy Spirit to really set one free. That's why Jesus said, in John 8:32, *"If the Son makes you free you will be free indeed."*

> **IT TAKES THE WORD OF GOD THROUGH THE POWER OF THE HOLY SPIRIT TO REALLY SET ONE FREE.**

In 1982 I tried to repeat the old hole-in-the-roof trick, as we had done years before at the Dollar Store. This time, a friend and I climbed the roof of a Western Clothing Store intending to cut a hole in the roof and go inside with a rope. Our intention was to steal all the high-dollar exotic skin boots and sell them on the black market. To our surprise, the roof had sensors that set off a silent alarm.

Before we could even get the hole in the roof cut, we were surrounded by Dallas Police officers. We went to jail, but I managed to get off on probation. Guess how I

Hellbound! Cancelled!

paid my crooked attorney? With exotic skin boots from a previous robbery. Crime was all I knew. Even when I held odd jobs, I always had crime on my mind.

At the time, Mom had a boyfriend she actually stayed with for several years. His nickname was Possum, and I'm pretty sure it was because he was the biggest thief anyone had ever known. Anyone who knew him can vouch for that fact.

Even though I was only seventeen, Possum would take me with him every morning around 5 o'clock to go steal construction machinery. Between the two of us, we would cut padlocks with a pair of huge bolt cutters and steal welding machines, diesel air compressors, big generators, and anything else left on trailers. Possum, of course, would only give me a fraction of his earnings from what we stole.

Chapter 7

Addicted Like My Elders

Because Mom and Possum were both alcoholics, I too got addicted to alcohol and then to cocaine. Sometime around 1981 my oldest sister Ida lived with a man who beat her, the same lifestyle we were all accustomed to. On one certain occasion, Mom butted in to their argument. She said that Ida's husband must be either gay or a coward because he only hit women. This made him so furious that he kicked Mom and was about to beat her.

Until this moment, I was standing outside, watching everything through the front screen door. I ran inside before he could beat Mom and stabbed him in the stomach with a big pocket knife I carried. He panicked and ran, but I chased him and stabbed him some more.

When the man fell to the ground motionless, my other brother-in-law dragged him into the car and took him to the hospital. They saved his life, and he didn't squeal on me. But that was pretty much the last time I ever saw him. He, too, continued a life of crime and finally died in a state prison years later.

In 1985, I committed the worst violent crime of my life. I will talk about in the last chapter of this book. I ran from the law and ended up back in Dallas. It was now 1986, and I met up with Mom and Possum again. By now Possum had graduated to selling big quantities of drugs. Nobody really trusted him, so he talked me into doing his dirty work for him.

Possum's connection would give him $100,000 at a time, and Possum would hand it to me so I could go get the drugs. The drug dealer didn't trust Possum but was willing to work through me because he was my sister Ida's boyfriend. They weren't paying me much, so I lied to Possum and the drug dealer and started making money off of both of them. It was a dog-eat-dog world.

On one occasion, my dealer was out of town when the buyer came in from North Carolina. Possum gave me the money, and I went to another dealer I knew down the road. The day passed, and the drugs had not yet arrived. The buyer got nervous and asked Mom to call me.

Mom called me at the other dealer's house, and the buyer (who was with Mom at the time) got on the phone. He asked me if his money was in my possession. I told him the drugs had been delayed and his money was safe with me. He was very nervous and full of doubt and questioned if I should continue to wait.

In the end, he told me to just head back to the hotel with his money. I brought him back his $100,000 in cash, and that day he learned that he could trust me and depend on me with his money or drugs. I seemed to be an honest thief.

I SEEMED TO BE AN HONEST THIEF.

Chapter 8

Keeping All the Wrong Company

Right around this time, between drug deals, I went to a party with a so-called friend. An argument started between my friend and another guy (over a dog, believe it or not). Anyway, this other guy was huge and well built. As they fought, I knew my friend couldn't handle the stock man, so I jumped on the guy's back and started hitting him with my knife handle. I never opened the knife, but I was able to cut his scalp badly with the big handle.

The big guy was obviously on drugs because he never went down. We got away and ran to the car, and this guy even followed us outside. He was a wild man, so we sped away.

Marty Perez

When my next drug deal came up, and Possum called, I refused to go. I was sure they were short-changing me because of my young age. Since the dealer didn't trust Possum, I began to execute my own plan to climb the ranks. The buyer pleaded with me to do the drug run for Possum, but I refused, and Possum went back home empty-handed.

When Possum could no longer get drugs for his buyer from North Carolina, he decided to contact me in private. The buyer offered me $10,000 to do the same runs I was previously doing for only $1,500. I immediately made a new best friend that day. I did a lot of these deals for this buyer during 1985 and 1986.

Around the middle of 1986, drugs became very scarce. Sometimes I would hold a buyer's money for months just to have it on hand if a deal popped up. Little deals would pop up here and there, but nothing seemed to me to be worth risking the buyers money. Believe it or not, in my ignorance, I would seek advice from so-called psychics. They would read tarot cards and tell me whether to go or not go to do a certain deal.

I also participated in witchcraft. A lady would anoint me with oil, give me a pill to swallow, and cleanse me with tree branches. How foolish I was! But this was what I had seen growing up, so I didn't know any better.

> **This was what I had seen growing up, so I didn't know any better!**

Chapter 9

A Close Call

It was during this dry, slow season that I decided to take my daughters to Disney World. The birth of Myra had been followed by the birth of Marissa and by that of Marlene. Martina would come along later. I adored these girls and was determined to take them to see Mickey Mouse and his friends.

The trip was arranged, but the day before leaving for Florida I got a call from a longtime family friend who was also in the drug business. He was in Houston and said he had a great deal, being that it was a dry season. It did seem like a great deal, and since I had known him for years, I told him

Marty Perez

I wanted in and would be there in about five hours.

Joe was working with me in the drug trade, and now he and I left Dallas with the intention of bringing the drugs from Houston back to Dallas that same day. I figured my guys could sell it for me while I took my kids to Florida.

Well, we got there, and my friend asked me to give his friend the money to go get the drugs and bring them back to the hotel. I knew who the guy was. He was a famous guitar player, but I didn't know him personally, so I said no. I would only do the deal if I could go with the guitar player.

We got to the place and got out of the car to go purchase the drugs, but we were ambushed as we rounded a corner. Three men with guns held me up and took my money bag.

The guitar player was instantly out of sight, and one of the guys left with the money bag. I was left alone with one man holding a gun to my head and the other man standing twenty feet away with his gun drawn.

Hellbound! Cancelled!

I told the man to let me go since I was unarmed and they had the money bag anyway. He said no, that he had to kill me. I don't know how or why, but the man dropped his gun, and we started to wrestle for it. The other gunman was pointing his gun but couldn't get a clear shot. Somehow I got away and ran as fast and as far as I could. I could hear gunshots behind me. They were both shooting at me.

That day I got away with my life and thought I must be Superman! Years later I acknowledge Who the real Super Hero was that saved my life that day. God knew that someday I would give my life to Christ, so He had been protecting me from death since I was a child. Wow!

> **YEARS LATER I ACKNOWLEDGE WHO THE REAL SUPER HERO WAS THAT SAVED MY LIFE THAT DAY!**

I am broken right now, just thinking that a Holy God would have His eye on such a violent criminal. I know that I deserved life in prison, and it is beyond me why God had mercy on me. He rescued me so many times when I should have died.

> **GOD RESCUED ME MANY TIMES WHEN I SHOULD HAVE DIED!**

Chapter 10

Recovering My Money

We ended up going to Disney World anyway, but I knew I had to get back to work. I had lost a lot of money, and I would have to find some way to recover it.

When I got back to Dallas and called my friend and the guitar player to threaten them, they knew I was crazy, so I was able to recover about half of the money I had lost in that drug deal gone bad.

Around this time, I went to Corpus Christi and a friend and I went out to a night club. He got in an argument with some guy, and I butted in. The guy asked me to step outside, and I said I would.

I turned to tell my friend where I was going, and the other guy took advantage and broke a beer bottle over the back of my head. He attempted to run away, but I caught up to him and stabbed him in the back of the neck. We then ran out the back door. Only God knows if he survived that knife wound.

Only God knows if the man survived that knife wound!

I went back to Dallas for business as usual. Mom and Possum were now at the end of their relationship. Mom moved to Garland, Texas and found an old friend, "Pacho La Changa." They became business partners running a home-based beer joint in that dry county. It was also a little Mexican whorehouse. Mom was crazy! As we were growing up, she would do anything at all to keep us from going hungry. She would beg, borrow, or steal to support me and my siblings. Yes, she would even prostitute herself.

The good thing is that shortly after I got saved, Mom also gave her life to the Lord. God transformed her life, and I got to witness that wonderful miracle. Hallelujah!

THE GOOD THING IS THAT SHORTLY AFTER I GOT SAVED, MOM ALSO GAVE HER LIFE TO THE LORD!

Once again, this time in Dallas, I went out with some friends, and I bad-mouthed the wrong guy at a local night club. This guy was big and pretty much dragged me outside. I jumped on him like a baby and gave him a bear hug. I knew not to let go or he would swat me around like a rag doll.

The bouncers separated us, but I was on the ground, and the guy was able to give me a good kick. Because I was so drunk, I didn't feel anything right then, but I sure felt it the next day, and the next. It's been thirty years now, and to this day, if I sleep on that side, my ribs still hurt me!

Right now, I want to thank God for His faithfulness. Thank You, Jesus, for Your grace and Your mercy! You kept me through it all!

Chapter 11

A Stolen Computer

I have to stop now to cry and wonder why a loving, perfect, holy God could love people like me. I don't fully understand why He would protect and rescue a violent criminal like myself time after time. Thank You, Jesus!

Now, back to my story.

One time, a friend and I went to see some girls at their apartment in Dallas. After we left and were in the car, I saw that the guy I was with had stolen the ladies' computer. He dropped me off and went home with his new computer. Well, the girls suspected that we had taken their computer, and they complained to some of the guys we knew. I had no idea they were friends with these girls.

Later on, I saw these guys at a party, and after they had drunk enough, they questioned me about the computer. I told them I had no part in the theft, but they forced me into their car at gunpoint. While they drove to my friend's house, one of the guys held a loaded shotgun to my side, so I wouldn't bail out on them.

When we got there, they walked me to the door at gunpoint, and I knocked on the door. Thank God my friend was home. He didn't open the door but asked why we were there. I told him the situation, and he told me that the computer was in the shed in the backyard. The guys got the computer, and we drove back to the party.

The men put their guns away and let me go as if nothing had happened. Again, God had rescued me by allowing my friend to be home, or I might very well have been killed.

Again, God had rescued me!

In the 1980s and 90s, between drug deals, I moved back and forth to Robstown and

Hellbound! Cancelled!

Dallas. One time seven or eight friends and I drove in two trucks to Robstown from Dallas. Somewhere near San Marcos, Texas, the other truck picked up two hitchhikers who joined them in the back of the truck.

We had no cellphones in those days, so I wondered why, somewhere in Odem, Texas, the other truck turned off onto a dirt road. We followed them down the dirt road for a good while until they finally pulled over. It turned out that the two hitchhikers they had picked up were teenaged girls who had run away from a detention center.

The girls seemed to be around fifteen years old, so I decided not to participate in what followed. I watched my friends rape those two girls and knew that I couldn't say or do anything about it. Then we all got on the trucks and headed to Robstown. One of the guys dropped off the girls somewhere in Corpus Christi, and that was the end of the whole affair ... as far as we were concerned.

Chapter 12

A Bank Robbery?

Next on the agenda was a bank robbery. A few years prior, a friend of mine had done a heist but eventually got caught. This time we had inside help and got away with it.

A few weeks after the robbery, I was questioned by Dallas law enforcement officers, but I denied knowing anything about it. Later, I learned that these same authorities had been involved in the bank robbery in some way or another without me knowing it.

I would like to point out that all the crimes I committed and the lifestyle I lived was caused by my alcohol and drug addictions. It all started when I drank a beer and smoked some weed, and then it escalated out of control.

Drug and alcohol abuse in my personal life was the main cause of me being a violent criminal. So I would say to even casual drinkers and drug users, "Quit while you're ahead!"

> **I would say to even casual drinkers and drug users, "Quit while you're ahead!"**

Not everyone who drinks or does drugs turns into a violent criminal, but other problems will most definitely occur, problems like infidelity, divorce, job insecurity, missing out on your children's activities, health issues, etc.

Some of these traits are passed down from generation to generation. Many call this a generational curse. It takes someone with courage to finally put a stop to such curses.

As I stated in the introduction, Dad's side of the family was crazy! One time two of his brothers were fighting, and one of them pulled a gun. My sister Ida and I were watching the fight, and saw when Uncle Pedro tried to shoot Uncle Danny. The bullet missed but went right through Ida's pants. It was a good thing she was wearing bell-bottoms! Shortly after this incident, both Uncle Pedro and Uncle Frank went to prison for murdering a local police officer.

Around this same time, two Mexican men showed up at my grandma's house. With my dad and uncles in prison, my cousins and siblings were easy targets, or so these guys thought.

Chapter 13

Uncle Benito's Plight

These two strange visitors were using one of our family members to stash drugs. Well, Joe and I found their stash of black tar heroin and stole it. Again, thank God we didn't get caught because the owners probably would have killed us.

On another note, Uncle Benito, another of Dad's brothers, had been paralyzed from the neck down for as long as I could remember. In his younger years, he had been an excellent boxer. Mom said that one time they were at a bar in Plainview, Texas, and Uncle Benito got into a fight and put a guy to sleep with one punch. The guy was on the floor snoring!

Marty Perez

When I was a kid, Uncle Benito would have me push him in his wheelchair to the local Cantina. There he would drink a few beers, score some weed, and then I would stroll him back home.

Uncle Benito also taught me how to cook heroin and had me shoot him up with it. Since I didn't know what I was doing, I would just stick him anywhere on his arms.

What a childhood! Obviously, all my stories don't fit into just one book, but I wanted to mention a few of my crazy uncles.

The reason Uncle Benito was paralyzed was that he was going to beat up a guy at a local bar, and the guy shot him in the neck.

Even while he was confined to bed, Uncle Benito was able to teach my cousin Joe how to box. Joe would go on to be a great boxer and even make it to the pros.

Going back to the 80s and 90s: Even though I was always on drugs and alcohol, I was able to save a few of my friends from drug overdoses. My friends David and

Chris both overdosed, and I was somehow able to keep them alive.

One older man died from a heroin overdose right in front of me at Grandma's house. I punched him in the chest over and over until he finally revived. Was this any kind of life?

WAS THIS ANY KIND OF LIFE?

Chapter 14

Plans to Kill Me

There were many more danger that God rescued me from. Earlier I mentioned one of the violent crimes I committed. Well, one of those people had a family member who was more violent than me. After his release from prison, he had plans to find me. It turned out that on his way, he got into a fight at a bar and was killed. I didn't realize that God had rescued me from this person until years later. But because I insisted on living a life of crime, my time to pay was fast approaching.

Because I insisted on living a life of crime, my time to pay was fast approaching!

In 1986, I went to Corpus to do a drug deal. I gave my supplier $100,000, but he got busted while picking up his load. With heavy pressure from my money guy, I was forced to find the stash house of my supplier. I hired two gunman, and we entered the house. My gunman tied up the homeowner, while I looked for the money.

The homeowner's fourteen-year-old daughter was present as well, but he chose not to harm her. I don't know how, but within five to ten minutes, we heard sirens in the distance. The three of us fled on foot to avoid being caught. I hid in a boat down the street.

After about thirty minutes, hoping the coast was clear, I walked down a random street and stopped at a house to ask for a ride. When I knocked on the door, a seventeen-year-old boy answered. I asked if he had jumper cables to help start my car. He said yes and went to his parents' bedroom. I followed him in, and he asked his dad for the keys and told him he was giving me a jump.

Hellbound! Cancelled!

You can imagine the look on the faces of this man and his wife as a total stranger was suddenly standing in their bedroom! Little did they know that I had a loaded gun on me. It was a good thing they didn't resist.

We got into the car, and I told the young man to take me to the 7-11 down the street instead. Then, to my surprise a police officer on foot jumped in front of us, which made the boy stop the car. When the boy saw that I had a gun, he got out of the car immediately, screaming, while I was taken down by the police.

I was arrested for aggravated robbery and spent the next three months in Nueces County Jail, awaiting trial. I finally managed to communicate with my money guy, and he bailed me out. I knew I needed quick cash for attorney fees, so I went back to Dallas two weeks later to look for a load to smuggle. I was able to get a hundred pounds of weed to load into the trunk of a car, and I headed for North Carolina.

Marty Perez

ARRESTED FOR AGGRAVATED ROBBERY, I SPENT THE NEXT THREE MONTHS IN NUECES COUNTY JAIL!

Chapter 15

Arrested in Arkansas

One day, while Joe and I and a family friend named Priscilla were driving east on I-40, I got pulled over in Loanoke, Arkansas. The police quickly found our stash of one hundred pounds of weed and took us to jail. On the way, I told Joe and Priscilla to follow my lead as we were being questioned.

I told the police that we were car transporters for used car lots. I said we were supposed to drop off the car at none other than Graceland in Memphis, Tennessee, and that we were just to park the car there and leave. They should bust the buyers, and that would prove our innocence.

Amazingly, the police believed my story and called in the FBI. We rode with the feds across the state line with their sniffing dog and high-tech equipment. An officer drove the other car.

They parked the car at Elvis Presley's mansion and waited for hours. When they saw that nobody was showing up to pick up the car, they took us back to jail in Arkansas.

It was 1986, and the small jail in Arkansas didn't have a computer. They had no idea that I was on bond for the aggravated robbery in Corpus Christi. So, they, too, released me on bond.

I finally went to court in Corpus and got six years state time for the aggravated robbery, and ended up at Central Unit in Sugarland, Texas.

While at Central Unit, I wrote a letter to Arkansas to tell them why I wouldn't be able to show up for court on the hundred pounds of weed. They also gave me six years, so I served both cases consecutively and got out after two years.

At Central Unit, I met a man among the many. He was serving a life sentence, but this guy was different from all the others.

Hellbound! Cancelled!

He was at peace, and it was very noticeable. I was curious, so he began to share with me where his peace came from. For the next two years or so, Sammy Rodriguez took his time to share the Word of God with me every chance he got.

I really liked the idea of being forgiven and gong to Heaven. However, surrendering my life and lifestyle to Jesus didn't sit nearly as well with me.

While at Central Unit, I worked in the guard's dry cleaners. One day, my coworker was going through the guard's clothes that had come in that day. Suddenly, about twenty packs of small sealed bags with marijuana in them came tumbling out. I pretended not to have seen anything. But I knew then that, although I liked Sammy's message, I just wasn't ready to change my lifestyle.

I got out of the Walls Unit in Huntsville, Texas, in late 1989 and went on to a halfway house in Houston.

CHAPTER 16

ORGANIZED CRIME

Sad, but true, I was back to my old ways again as soon as I was released from the Texas Department of Corrections. I worked some jobs just to comply with my parole, but soon started selling drugs on the side. When I was released from the Houston halfway house, I moved back to Dallas and continued the rat race.

My drinking and cocaine habit had gotten even worse than before. In 1991, my wife and I went to Cancun, Mexico on vacation, and the trip became a nightmare. While in Cancun, I got very drunk and began an argument with her. I was so demon controlled that I started to strangle her. Somehow, she got away and ran to the front desk of the resort. The next morning, I was very ashamed when I saw severe bruising on her neck.

All during this time, I was heavy into adultery and prostitutes. I had started an organized crime team to smuggle drugs to various states. We would send drugs through trains and buses.

One time, I sent several people on different buses with loads of drugs in new luggage. On the way back, they were to ditch the new luggage and carry the cash on their bodies. One of my guys made a huge mistake. Since the luggage was new, he wanted to keep a piece of it. He brought an empty suitcase with him on the plane, and immediately, the airport authorities were onto him.

When my guys arrived at the airport, all the men went to the rest room and put their money in a bag. The bag was given to my driver, and we waited for the next guy to exit the terminal.

As soon as he came out the door, he was approached by DEA officers. Of course, they questioned why he had an empty suitcase.

Hellbound! Cancelled!

One DEA officer questioned my driver, but I told him we weren't together, so he let her go. The driver parked in a nearby garage and took the airport shuttle to our stash house. I watched helplessly as the DEA questioned my guy.

They found $10,000 in cash on his body. I don't know if he was stealing from me or just hadn't had time to put the money in the bag. Maybe he was nervous because he knew the DEA was onto him? Needless to say, I never saw that guy again.

During this time, my brother Tommy, and I opened Perez Paint & Body Shop in Lewisville, Texas. Of course, it was mainly a front. With the drug money, I bought a nice house in Colony, Texas. All my neighbors believed I was in the car business—which I was. But, like the body shop, it was only a front.

ALL MY NEIGHBORS BELIEVED I WAS IN THE CAR BUSINESS—WHICH I WAS. BUT, LIKE THE BODY SHOP, IT WAS ONLY A FRONT!

Chapter 17

Where Was I?

My Drug and alcohol addiction was so bad now that I would literally black out at times. One time I woke up in a strange house and had absolutely no idea where I was.

Not only was I living this terrible lifestyle; I also encouraged my siblings to do the same. Whenever possible, I would include them in my drug dealings. My siblings and I would also go out to nightclubs or house parties together. We would drink and do drugs together and sometimes even include our parents. It was that bad!

Sadly, my sister Ida did some bad coke that was laced with who knows what. She had a stroke and was left partially paralyzed. She never fully recovered and had to get around in a wheelchair. She died a few years later. It's important to note that even though Ida didn't die of a stroke, ultimately the cause of her death was drug abuse. My dad also died in 1991 from liver failure due to heroine abuse.

Please be aware that drugs don't always kill people right away. My dad abused drugs for many years before his liver failed. I was on drugs and alcohol for at least fifteen to twenty years, but by the grace of God I made it out alive. That's not always the case. So, if you're abusing drugs or alcohol, please seek help before it's too late.

If you're abusing drugs or alcohol, please seek help before it's too late!

Yes, there are programs out there that can help. In my case, I was too hard-headed for Alcoholics Anonymous. It wasn't enough for me. It took a supernatural visit from God to shake me at the very core of my being in order for me to listen.

It took a supernatural visit from God to shake me at the very core of my being in order for me to listen!

Before this could happen, one of the last drug deals I did was with my cousin/brother Joe. He went to pick up a load of drugs for me, and on the way back he got pulled over by the police. He was arrested but was out of jail in a year or so.

While Joe was in jail, he planned his revenge on the guy he knew had set him up. Upon his release, we went out to celebrate and got wasted. We left the club and headed to the man's house to do a drive-by shooting!

Chapter 18

Closing In

I learned that the feds were closing in on me and my brother Tommy, so we left our home and body shop and went to hide out in McAllen, Texas, for a while. A few months later, when things seemed to have cooled off, we went back home and continued our wicked way of living.

One morning I woke up at home, not able to remember how we had gotten home from the club. My wife told me I had driven home, but I didn't remember that at all. She was crying and told me I had acted a fool the night before. She told me that she was so tired of me she wished she'd had the guts to kill me in my sleep. She said that I was so evil and mean she just couldn't take it anymore.

Marty Perez

Later that morning, I went into the living room to lie on the couch. The drug and alcohol poisoning in my body had reached such a level that I felt like I was about to die. As I lay there motionless, I could hear the voice of an evangelist on TV. His name was Robert Tilton, and he seemed to be talking about the exact things I was going through. It was as if he had already read this book (which I would not write until twenty-five years later).

Because I couldn't move, I was forced to just lie there and listen to this message. I knew right there and then that if I didn't start making better choices, my life would soon be over. At that moment I wept, and reality set in. I was nothing but a violent career criminal, a hopeless addict. I desperately needed help. Since I really didn't know how to pray, I just said, "God, help me!"

> **SINCE I REALLY DIDN'T KNOW HOW TO PRAY, I JUST SAID, "GOD, HELP ME!"**

I survived, and a few weeks later went to a party in Robstown. The following morning, while driving to a store to get some beer to ease my hangover, I got pulled over by a state trooper. I had let my inspection sticker expire (what a smart criminal, huh?).

The trooper asked for my driver's license, then came back and asked me to get out of the car. He placed me under arrest, saying that I had a pending federal arrest warrant out of North Carolina. I went before a federal judge in Nueces County and was charged by U.S. Customs for drug trafficking. My life as I had known it was over.

My journey to North Carolina from Corpus Christi took about a month, going from county jail to county jail. My brother Tommy had been arrested the month before, so he was already at the Mecklenburg County Jail in Charlotte, North Carolina.

Chapter 19

Who Came into My Cell?

About a week after I arrived in Charlotte, I was lying on my bunk just pondering my life. I had a blanket over my face, but I felt someone come into the small cell. I sat up and looked around, but no one was there.

> **I SAT UP AND LOOKED AROUND, BUT NO ONE WAS THERE!**

I lay back down and covered my face again, and again I felt someone come into the cell. But, when I looked, again, no one was there!

The first thing I thought was that the Grim Reaper himself had come to take me to Hell. I waited nervously, but nothing happened.

When I had waited some more, I began to feel a sense of peace.

Now, I was starting to think about the Word that Sammy Rodriguez had shared with me five years before at TDC. When you share the Word of God, it doesn't always bear fruit immediately.

WHEN YOU SHARE THE WORD OF GOD IT DOESN'T ALWAYS BEAR FRUIT IMMEDIATELY!

Sammy had patiently shared the Gospel of Jesus Christ with me, and it had taken five years to germinate. There in that tiny cell I got on my knees and asked God to forgive me for my life of crime and violence. I was doubtful that a holy God could even think about forgiving a person like me, who had done so many terrible things. Nevertheless, I had nothing to lose. \

I asked the Lord to come into my heart and gave Him permission to do with my life whatever He wanted. I said, "Lord, if You can save and change an evil savage like me, please go ahead."

Hellbound! Cancelled!

I didn't hear or see anything weird or mystical, but I knew beyond a shadow of a doubt that something supernatural had just taken place in my heart. I felt a joy and a peace that I had never experienced before. Thank you, Sammy Rodriguez, wherever you are.

Since Tommy was at a federal detention center down the street, I wanted to share my experience with him. I immediately wrote him a letter and gave it to the mail guy when he came by later that day.

As I was giving the mailman my letter, he was also giving me a letter from Tommy. I immediately opened the letter and began to read. To my amazement, Tommy said that he had given his life to the Lord! Wow, I could hardly believe that God had reached both of us about the same time.

God had reached both of us about the same time!

A few weeks later, I was transferred to the federal facility where Tommy was. He was

Marty Perez

about a hundred yards away in a different POD, but we could see each other through the chain-link fence. What a joy that was!

Chapter 20

Spending Time Mopping the Hall

The prison guard in my dorm was a Christian and knew my brother was down the hall. He was friends with the guard over that section, who was also a Christian. The two guards coordinated to allow me and Tommy to mop the hallway at the same time. That's was where we could talk and spend a little time together.

We both asked the chaplain if he would allow us to call our mom from his office. He said yes and scheduled a day. At that time, we had only been saved a couple of months and knew nothing about the Bible or ministry. After the phone call to Mom, the chaplain began to talk to us. Then, he took out a small bottle of oil, put some of it on our heads, and prayed for us.

In his prayer, the chaplain was saying that God was going to use Tommy and me in ministry and in preaching the Word. At the time, we thought this guy was off his rocker. What was he smoking? But a few short years later, his prophecy would come true. Both of us began working in ministry and preaching the Word of God. Hallelujah!

A FEW SHORT YEARS LATER, HIS PROPHECY CAME WOULD COME TRUE. BOTH OF US BEGAN WORKING IN MINISTRY AND PREACHING THE WORD OF GOD!

After the prayer with the chaplain that day, we each went back to our own dorm. Then I met a guy in my dorm by the name of Raymond Gribble, and he invited me to read the Bible there at one of the small dinner tables in our dorm. I agreed, but then he came back the next day, and the next! There was no stopping this guy because we were in the same dorm, and I had nowhere to hide. So, we read the Bible every day for four or five hours a day, and I soon began to understand some familiar Bible passages.

This continued for ten months, and can you imagine what happened? I got hooked on reading the Bible. For the first time in my life I was addicted to something that was actually good for me (see 1 Corinthians 16:15 and Acts 6:4).

After my ten months in the detention center, I was sentenced to six years in federal prison and was sent to Beckley, West Virginia. I never saw Raymond Gribble again, but God had used him to get me hooked on the Word. Thank you, Raymond, wherever you are.

Chapter 21

Attending a Spanish-Speaking Church

At Beckley I was invited to a Spanish church service. I had never attended a Spanish service before, but I went anyway. I soon discovered that what we had learned at home in Robstown growing up was not really Spanish, but Spanglish. I had a lot to learn. I ended up helping in that ministry for the few short months I was there.

Before I left Beckley, the chaplain asked to talk to me. He said that in all his years in prison ministry, many of the inmates have vowed to serve God and work in the ministry. But for him this would be the first time he was reaching out to an inmate. He told me that he felt God had a call on my life and asked if I would take some correspondence courses free of charge. I said yes and did all of the training courses in a quarter of the time allowed.

After West Virginia, I was transferred to a federal prison in Beaumont, Texas. I stayed in another county jail before Beaumont for a whole month. The door to that cell had a gap at the bottom, and that was where they would slide my plate of food to me. It was almost as if I was distant from the rest of the world, and nobody knew where I was. They would only allow me out of that cell for one hour a day for a shower and a short walk. It didn't matter because by then I had already read most of the Bible and knew that God would never leave me nor forsake me.

> **It didn't matter because by then I had already read most of the Bible and knew that God would never leave me nor forsake me!**

Hellbound! Cancelled!

Somehow they missed a pocket-sized Gideon Bible I had in my possession. I read and prayed in a one-man cell for that whole month. It wasn't a federal jail, so I was on lock down twenty-four hours a day.

One day, while I was praying, I literally felt that God stepped into that cell with me. I had my eyes closed, but His presence was so tangible. It was as if I could almost touch Him.

I opened my eyes very slowly, thinking that He would let me see His glory. I didn't see Him, but His presence was enough to let me know that He was making Himself available to me.

As I stood there in awe, God showed me myself standing on a stairway. He told me to take a step upward, and when I did, the steps beneath me disappeared. God showed me that as long as I sought Him, He would always elevate me to higher levels in my walk with Christ.

GOD SHOWED ME THAT AS LONG AS I SOUGHT HIM, HE WOULD ALWAYS ELEVATE ME TO HIGHER LEVELS IN MY WALK WITH CHRIST!

Chapter 22

A Well-Organized Church

When I got to the Beaumont Federal Prison, I started attending English services. They were led by the chaplain of the facility, and they were just like a regular service in a church on the outside. The chaplain and his inmate leaders had musical instruments for worship, they had prayer, they served communion, and they had altar calls. This group was very well set up.

I then started attending the Spanish services at this same facility. This group did not have a chaplain, so they conducted their own services through the use of inmates.

Marty Perez

They were set up with an inmate pastor and other inmate leadership.

After a few short weeks of me attending this group, the inmate pastor asked if I would do the announcements at the Spanish service. I did the announcements and then begin to participate with the Spanish group quite frequently.

After several months, the Spanish leaders asked if I would be interested in joining their leadership team. Sometime later, because of some problems in the Spanish ministry, the prison chaplain stepped in and made some changes. A different inmate leader was voted in to be our new pastor, and I was voted in to be the co-pastor. This was in 1998.

Interestingly enough, the brother who became our new pastor is now pastor of his own ministry in his home country of Colombia. Hallelujah!

During the five years I was in federal prison, I had many great spiritual experiences and was able to grow spiritually. Whether we were in services or in the recreation yard, we prayed for inmates who were sick, and God would heal them on the spot.

> **WHETHER WE WERE IN SERVICES OR IN THE RECREATION YARD, WE PRAYED FOR INMATES WHO WERE SICK, AND GOD WOULD HEAL THEM ON THE SPOT!**

On one occasion, a certain man came to the Spanish leaders and told us his story. He said that he had been a satanic priest but was nervous about telling us. He said he was tired of the cult and wanted out, but he was afraid what they might try to do to him. We asked him to come to our next Sunday service so that we could pray for him in private.

The Spanish leaders had set up a private prayer room in a large mop closet. While worship music was on, we took this man in the closet to pray for him. As we prayed for him, we literally heard bells and figured it was because of his occultic priestly position.

As God delivered the man through our prayers of faith, we heard screams like those of a goat. I really don't know what it all meant, but I do know that God set that man free, and he then became a member of our church. Hallelujah!

CHAPTER 23

DOING EVANGELISM

We also did evangelism in the rec yard, the chow hall, and the individual dorms. At times we would all pitch in to make a spread in the commissary and then take it out to the rec yard to share with the other men. There we set up the food and cokes and then called out for everyone to come and eat.

Once we had a good-sized group gathered, I would ask them to bow their heads for prayer. I stood on a picnic table to pray, and before the prayer, I took five or ten minutes to share the Gospel. It was great because we had a captive audience. Jesus did the same thing, we figured, so why not us?

The other leaders and I were honored to lead many inmates to salvation through faith in Christ, and the satisfaction this brought was priceless!

> **THE OTHER LEADERS AND I WERE HONORED TO LEAD MANY INMATES TO SALVATION THROUGH FAITH IN CHRIST, AND THE SATISFACTION THIS BROUGHT WAS PRICELESS!**

One evening, as I walked through the compound, I stopped and looked up to Heaven. I smiled and told God, Thank You, because I had never felt so free in my life. In my mind I was thinking, How is it possible that I feel so free when I am locked up in prison? Well, my body was in a prison, but my spirit man was finally free. Hallelujah!

During those days in prison, I was able to forgive my dad for putting Mom, myself, and my siblings through a living Hell for so many years, and God gave me a love for him that I had never felt before. Even though he had passed away years before, I was free to love him anyway.

The truth is that I chose to forgive my dad and everyone else who had caused me pain or sorrow in the past. I also asked God to forgive *me* for all the people I had hurt and the lives I had damaged. God not only forgave me; I was also freed from all guilt and condemnation.

In 1998 I met Antonio, a young man (he was twenty-two at the time) who had come to prison for the first time. He had never before been convicted of a crime. Antonio said that all his family members were Christians, but he had veered off on the wrong path. I talked to my counselor and managed to get Antonio moved to my dorm and two-man cubicle. I took him under my wing, knowing that he was a first-timer.

Antonio and I became really close friends, so much so that he even began to call me Dad.

On one occasion, my youngest sister, Carolina, brought my daughters to visit me in Beaumont. Antonio had asked his mother Carmen to come visit him, and she arrived that same day. In this way, we met each others' families and had a great visit.

Marty Perez

After this, Antonio told me to put his mother on my visiting list as well, so that when she came to visit him, I could tag along. After meeting Carmen and seeing how beautiful she was, I said, "Absolutely!"

Getting a visit in prison was like taking a kid to a candy store. From then on, Antonio's mom came to visit him nearly every weekend. Her visits were, for us, like being in Heaven. Then a funny thing happened. Well, for me, it was good, not really funny.

> **GETTING A VISIT IN PRISON WAS LIKE TAKING A KID TO A CANDY STORE!**

Chapter 24

Getting to Know Carmen

When Carmen would come to visit, she wouldn't always sign for her son, Antonio, to come to the visiting room. This allowed me to spend several hours visiting with her and getting to know her. I liked what I saw, and we soon developed a strong bond.

I was finally released from Federal Prison on July 5, 2000, just one day after Independence Day. I had been free spiritually, but now I was free physically.

Upon release, I had to report to a half-way house in Dallas and stay there for six months. After I finished my time at the half-way house, I want to stay with my daughters in a lovely Texas town known as The Colony.

Marty Perez

After my arrest, most of my ill-gotten wealth was confiscated by the government, so I would have to start life over again. As soon as I was able to travel within the state of Texas, I asked Joe to take me to Houston to see Carmen. My first wife had renounced me while I was in prison, and we had been divorced.

Once together, Carmen and I didn't want to be apart. After months of being together, we were married. Yes, I married my cellmate's mom, whom I met in a federal prison visiting room. God moves His chess pieces in strategic ways to assure His victory.

Carmen and I have now been married for eighteen years, and we have a sixteen-year-old daughter, who is also serving the Lord.

After attending several different churches, we moved to Katy, Texas, and started going to Powerhouse Christian Center. There we served in the Spanish ministry for about three years. We helped the Spanish pastor with the teaching and assisted with the encounters and church events.

In January of 2006 we moved to New Orleans to work in the aftermath of

Hellbound! Cancelled!

Hurricane Katrina. There we started attending a Spanish ministry named El Verbo (the Word). After six months with this congregation, we were assigned as homegroup leaders. I was also a big part of the evangelism team.

The aftermath of Katrina presented some unique opportunities. There were always several hundred men (most of them Spanish speaking) at the building material stores looking for work, and I began to take food, water, clothes, and shoes to them there. I would stand on the roof of our church van and preach the Gospel to them. Then, after praying with the men, we would hand out the food and supplies.

On one occasion, we prayed for a man who seemed to be demon possessed. His friends saw us out there, so they came and asked us to go to this man's house. When we got there, the man was wielding a knife and screaming obscenities. Our team finally calmed him down long enough to pray for him.

After prayer, the man looked like a totally different person. Years later, this man contacted us to thank us and let us know that he was doing well. He had bought a truck and was now running his own business. God is so good!

> **AFTER PRAYER, THE MAN LOOKED LIKE A TOTALLY DIFFERENT PERSON!**

CHAPTER 25

A New Ministry out of the Rubble

Because of the damage done by Hurricane Katrina, hundreds of men had flocked to the New Orleans area looking for work. They stood on the street corners waiting for someone to come along and pick them up for a day of labor. Our team started looking for a place to minister to these people, a place out of the weather.

One local hotel offered us a conference room to use for that ministry. God also had other provision for us. When our senior pastor told a pastor friend of his what we were doing on the streets of New Orleans, this pastor said we could use a large upper room at his church. The advantages were that this space also had a kitchen, and his church was within walking distance of the hotel we were planning to use. We began Tuesday night meetings and allowed as many as could fit in to come. We first served a hot dinner to those who came, and then we preached the Gospel to them. Our guests were mostly men, although we occasionally had some women and children too.

This Tuesday night ministry went on for the next six years. Hallelujah! Many lives were touched with the Gospel and the love of God through our volunteers.

MANY LIVES WERE TOUCHED WITH THE GOSPEL AND THE LOVE OF GOD THROUGH OUR VOLUNTEERS!

Those volunteers were too many to count, but I would like to thank a few who served for those six years of salvations, miracles, signs and wonders. Thank you Dr. Soto, Cesar, Manuel and Manuela, and Hombres al Maximo, just to name a few.

Hellbound! Cancelled!

Because of Hurricane Katrina, two of the families from our church had relocated to Hammond, Louisiana, on the other side of Lake Pontchartrain from New Orleans. Along with these two families, one of our pastors started a homegroup in Hammond that grew into a small congregation, and Carmen and I assisted him. Again, God opened a door for us to start meetings at a local church.

A few months into that ministry, our pastor in Hammond was called to move back to New Orleans because of a new church that was starting up on what is called the West Bank of New Orleans, and Carmen and I were left in charge of the small congregation in Hammond.

We pastored that church for two years and then were brought back to the mother church in Kenner, just outside of New Orleans.

Once the West Bank church opened, one of our other pastors was sent there, and I asked to be transferred and was allowed to join him and his team.

Soon afterward, the senior pastor of the new church in the West Bank asked me to join his team of pastors. For me, that was a great honor and one of the most memorable highlights of those eleven years in New Orleans. We served there for four years and experienced the glory of God. Thank you, Haroldo, for giving me that opportunity. Special thanks to Ron Reid as well.

> **FOR ME, THAT WAS A GREAT HONOR AND ONE OF THE MOST MEMORABLE HIGHLIGHTS OF THOSE ELEVEN YEARS IN NEW ORLEANS!**

CHAPTER 26

HOMBRES AL MAXIMO

My brother Tommy and I, along with Pastor Harold and other leaders, started a men's ministry known as Hombres al Maximo. That ministry is still alive and active today. Because of HAM, I was invited to preach the Gospel at a local high school. I had gotten my GED in prison, but had never been inside a high school before. I am so grateful to God for all the ministry opportunities.

> **I AM SO GRATEFUL TO GOD FOR ALL THE MINISTRY OPPORTUNITIES!**

For almost twenty years, since my release from federal prison, I have participated in ministry in many arenas. By the grace of God, I have seen marriages restored, alcohol and drug addicts delivered, demons cast out, homosexuals come to Christ, and sick folk healed. All glory be to God! I am so grateful that although I had been a perverted man and a violent criminal, God still chose to use me (see 1 Corinthians 1:26).

After Hurricane Harvey impacted the Houston area, Carmen, Isabella, and I moved to Baytown, Texas, and became part of an awesome church there in Mont Belvieu for two years, under Pastor Don Gibson.

We still participated in ministry as much as my job allowed. My dream was to make my business so successful that it would allow me to manage my own time. That way, I could be free to serve God more and more. For the time being, I was one of the captains on the usher team at the church.

I had also been approved by the Texas Department of Corrections to participate in preaching the Gospel to inmates at their facilities. As I shared my story and the grace of God, the inmates at TDC had an instant connection with me, knowing that I had been in their shoes. Some of them were in shock when they heard my testimony because I did things in my past that were way worse than what they had ever done. This got their attention. If God could forgive and use a person like me, then they, too, certainly had hope. Hallelujah!

IF GOD COULD FORGIVE AND USE A PERSON LIKE ME, THEN THEY, TOO, CERTAINLY HAD HOPE!

I had never thought I would return to TDC, but when I did, thirty years after my release, it felt weird being behind the barbed wired. But the experience was second to none. Men who were there could see the Light of the Gospel from a different prospective because they related to me one-on-one.

I shared with these men everything I have written in this book, and they knew that I could identify with what they had gone through and were going through—the hurt, the pain, the rejection, the addictions, the abuse, and all the rest. Thank God, I was able to show them a way of escape.

Chapter 27

Why I Wrote the Book

In 2006, I began a home remodeling business. It was successful and I did well for many years. Then I began working at oil and gasoline refineries. When the Covid Pandemic struck, there were many layoffs. Then, when I went back to work, I injured my back and had to spend some months in rehab. This forced me to concentrate on the invention of some new products that I hope will hit the market soon.

After Hurricane Ida struck the coast of Louisiana in 2021 and moved inland, devastating many communities, Carmen and I returned to that state to help with the rebuilding efforts. That's where we find ourselves as this book goes to press.

I have shared everything in this book for a reason. To everyone and anyone who feels they will never amount to anything or can never succeed in business, marriage, or ministry, I say, "There is hope for you."

Psalm 37:5 and Proverbs 16:3 tell us to put all of our ideas and efforts into God's hands, trust in Him, and He will do the rest to help us succeed. Do not allow your past to determine your future.

Do not allow your past to determine your future!

Proverbs 3:5-6 says, *"Trust in the LORD with all your heart and don't rely on your own understanding. In all your ways acknowledge Him and He will direct your paths."* I am a witness to the fact that this works.

As long as I live, I will continue to proclaim the Gospel of Jesus Christ and the goodness of God. I do this, not only behind a pulpit, but also in the marketplace and workplace. My platform is wherever I go. I am not ashamed of the Gospel, for through

Hellbound! Cancelled!

it and because of it, I am alive today!

I want to take this opportunity to thank God for restoring my relationship with four of my daughters: Myra, Marissa, Marlene, and Martina. I had, at one time, destroyed my relationship with them through my ignorance and continual criminal life. But our God is a God of restoration, and it is never too late to be restored to our loved ones. Yes, there is hope for you too.

I have so many more accounts that I could write about, but they are full of the same perversions, adulteries, and violence. And, since my real intention is to glorify the God of salvation and restoration, I believe and hope I have brought my point across. To God be all the glory!

> **SINCE MY REAL INTENTION IS TO GLORIFY THE GOD OF SALVATION AND RESTORATION, I BELIEVE AND HOPE I HAVE BROUGHT MY POINT ACROSS!**

Now I would like to end this chapter with a funny but true story. When I met my wife, Carmen, she had three grown children: Sylvia, Antonio, and Valerie. Back in 1998, when my brother Tommy brought my daughters to visit me in Beaumont, he not only met my wife-to-be; he also met my wife's oldest daughter, Sylvia. A few years after I married Carmen, Tommy married Sylvia, and together they have two sons, Michael and Joshua. These are Carmen's biological grandchildren, but they are my nephews. However, they call Grandpa because I am married to their grandmother. Isn't God good!

Chapter 28

That Terrible Crime

In the early pages of this book, I spoke of a terrible crime I had committed and promised that I would tell you about it the final pages of the book. I want to keep that promise.

My first wife and I were separated at one point, and she told me that I could not see my daughters. During a certain drunk spell, I went to her mom's house, where my wife was staying, broke down the door, and started cutting her with a knife.

Hearing the commotion, her mom came into the room, and to my disgrace, I stabbed her in the chest. It was, to my way of thinking, the worst crime I ever committed.

I say that it is the worst, not only because it was committed against two helpless women, but also because neither of them deserved that. My ex-wife and I had many differences and had sinned against each other many time. Her mother, however, had always been very kind to me, treating me like a son.

Both my ex-wife and her mother were taken to the hospital. My ex-wife required many stitches, and her mother had to be hospitalized because of her wounds.

They were interviewed by the police and a warrant was immediately issued for my arrest. I was forced to flee the area and lay low until things could blow over.

Thankfully, my wife and her mother both survived. My ex-wife and I actually got together again after that, and all the charges against me were dropped. But what a terrible thing I did! Strong drink and drugs drive us to terrible crimes.

STRONG DRINK AND DRUGS DRIVE US TO TERRIBLE CRIMES.

As I conclude this short testimony, I pray

that this message will bring hope to many. If you or anybody you know feels hopeless, hurt, rejected, misunderstood, or even on the verge of suicide, please know this: Our only hope is in Jesus Christ. You may be going through separation or divorce, sickness or disease, alcohol or drug addiction. No matter what it is, first cry out to God, and then seek help from others.

Our only hope is in Jesus Christ!

God's desire is for all to be saved. 2 Peter 3:9 says that God is patient with us, not wanting anyone to be destroyed, but wanting everyone to repent.

Maybe you have not been an evil person like I was, or maybe you have been or are even worse than me. Whatever your situation, God is still your answer. Romans 5:20 says that where sin is massive, God's grace is even bigger than our sin.

Please pray the following prayer with me:

Marty Perez

Father God,

I come before You in the name of Jesus. I believe that Jesus died on the cross and that You raised Him from the dead on the third day. Please forgive me of all the sins I have committed. Jesus, come into my heart and save my soul. I receive You as my Lord and Savior. Help me to become the person You created me to be. Help me to live for You, so that I can also help others to know You and Your forgiveness.

**In Jesus name,
Amen!**

After you have finished with this book, please pass it on to someone else who might be in need of God's grace and mercy.

Chapter 29

In Closing

Now, in closing, I would like to give a shout-out to brothers Montes, Benavides, Hammer, Justo, Winston, Miguelito, Boy, Sam, Jhon Jairo, Alonzo, Luis, and all the brothers with whom I spent five years at Beaumont Federal Prison.

AUTHOR CONTACT PAGE

You may contact Marty Perez directly for speaking engagements in the following ways:

eMail: mperez1264@yahoo.com

Phone: 832-322-5757

www.ingramcontent.com/pod-product-compliance
Lightning Source LLC
LaVergne TN
LVHW011204080426
835508LV00007B/590